JAMMIN'
WITH THE JONAS BROTHERS

AN UNAUTHORIZED BIOGRAPHY BY LEXI RYALS

PRICE STERN SLOAN
Published by the Penguin Group
Penguin Group (USA) Inc., 375 Hudson Street, New York, New York 10014, USA
Penguin Group (Canada), 90 Eglinton Avenue East, Suite 700, Toronto, Ontario M4P
2Y3, Canada
(a division of Pearson Penguin Canada Inc.)
Penguin Books Ltd., 80 Strand, London WC2R 0RL, England
Penguin Group Ireland, 25 St. Stephen's Green, Dublin 2, Ireland
(a division of Penguin Books Ltd.)
Penguin Group (Australia), 250 Camberwell Road, Camberwell, Victoria 3124, Australia
(a division of Pearson Australia Group Pty. Ltd.)
Penguin Books India Pvt. Ltd., 11 Community Centre, Panchsheel Park, New Delhi—110
017, India
Penguin Group (NZ), 67 Apollo Drive, Rosedale, North Shore 0632, New Zealand
(a division of Pearson New Zealand Ltd.)
Penguin Books (South Africa) (Pty.) Ltd., 24 Sturdee Avenue,
Rosebank, Johannesburg 2196, South Africa

Penguin Books Ltd., Registered Offices: 80 Strand, London WC2R 0RL, England

Photo credits: Cover: courtesy of Eric Shimohata/Prphotos.com; Insert Photos: first page
courtesy of Janet Mayer/Prphotos.com; second page courtesy of Eric Shimohata/
Prphotos.com; Anthony Moore/Prphotos.com; third page courtesy of Eric Shimohata/
Prphotos.com; Eric Shimohata/Prphotos.com; Eric Shimohata/Prphotos.com; fourth page
courtesy of Eric Shimohata/Prphotos.com

Library of Congress Cataloging-in-Publication Data

Ryals, Lexi.
Jammin' with the Jonas Brothers : an unauthorized biography / by Lexi Ryals.
p. cm.
ISBN 978-0-8431-3304-2 (pbk.)
1. Jonas Brothers (Musical group)--Juvenile literature. 2. Rock musicians--
United States--Biography--Juvenile literature. I. Title. II. Title: Jamming with
the Jonas Brothers.
ML3930.J62R93 2008
782.42164092'2--dc22
[B]

2007044932

ISBN 978-0-8431-3304-2   10 9 8 7 6 5 4 3 2 1

JAMMIN' WITH THE JONAS BROTHERS

N UNAUTHORIZED BIOGRAPHY BY LEXI RYALS

PSS!
PRICE STERN SLOAN

CONTENTS

INTRODUCTION

MEET THE JONAS BROTHERS

March 1, 2006, was a chilly day in New York City, but things were heating up in MTV Studios, where Total Request Live was getting ready to film. The studio audience was full of excited high school girls, not to mention the four hundred fans camped out on the sidewalk below. They were all there because one of their favorite bands was making an appearance on the show that day.

Filming began and everyone cheered as the videos for fan favorites like the Pussycat Dolls' "Beep," Aly & AJ's "Rush," Kanye West's "Touch the Sky," and Ashlee Simpson's "L.O.V.E." were played. But no one in the audience was as excited as the three brothers waiting in the wings. Kevin, Joseph, and Nick Jonas were about to watch the video for their first single, "Mandy," have its world premiere. Then they were giving an interview with one of TV's hottest VJs. These were pretty big steps for the three teenage brothers from New Jersey.

Finally the moment the boys had been waiting for arrived. Vanessa Minnillo, one of TRL's hosts and a certified hottie, announced the world premiere of the brand-spankin'-new video from the Jonas Brothers. The band's pop-punk, high-energy music filled the studio as their first-ever music video lit up the screen. The brothers were probably pretty nervous as they waited for the crowd to react, but they didn't have anything to worry about. As the last few notes of "Mandy" died away, the crowd went wild.

After a quick commercial break, the Jonas Brothers took the stage. The boys smiled and waved as they were introduced.

"This is get to know the Jonas Brothers," Vanessa announced. She quizzed the boys on their passions, musical influences, female fans, and rejection—and they answered every question like pros. But it was the youngest band member, Nick, who stole the show with his smooth moves.

"Nicholas, who do you think are the sexiest sisters: the Olsens, the Duffs, or the Hiltons?" Vanessa asked him.

"Um. Do you have a sister?" Nick answered sheepishly, flashing Vanessa a shy smile. His brothers whooped and gave Nick high fives as the girls in the audience let out a resounding, "Awwwwwww."

The brothers smiled at each other, drinking in the crowd's response. They had finally arrived.

CHAPTER 1
GROWING UP JONAS

When Paul and Denise Jonas got married, they probably never imagined that one day their sons would be rocking out on MTV. Paul Kevin Jonas Sr. and his wife, Denise, started their life together in the small town of Teaneck, New Jersey. They were both musicians who had dedicated their lives to spreading the message of Christianity. Denise was proficient in sign language, and she and her husband went from church to church, leading worship programs for the hearing impaired.

Denise and Paul were very much in love and ready to start a family. So when Denise discovered she was going to have a baby early in 1987, they rejoiced. They continued their ministry work until Denise became too big for the road. On November 5, 1987, she gave birth to Paul Kevin Jonas II. The happy couple called their new son Kevin so he wouldn't be confused with his dad. Luckily, baby Kevin was pretty easygoing, because his parents weren't content to remain in New Jersey for long.

Shortly after Kevin was born, the Jonas family went back on the road to continue spreading the Christian message. Kevin loved traveling with his parents, although he must have gotten a little lonely with no playmates his own age around. But Kevin wouldn't be alone much longer. When he was only one year old, Denise discovered she was expecting again, although that didn't slow her down. She continued to travel with Paul and Kevin through the summer.

The family was in sunny Arizona on August 15, 1989, when Denise gave birth to her second son. The proud parents named their new arrival Joseph Adam Jonas, or Joe for short. Kevin must have been pretty excited to become a big brother!

As the two boys grew older, it soon became clear

that Denise and Paul were going to have their hands full with the two rambunctious toddlers. Kevin was a thoughtful and sensitive child, but he was also excellent at convincing his baby brother to get into mischief. Joe's reckless sense of adventure would later earn him the nickname "Danger" within the family.

Kevin and Joseph loved playing games together. Maybe it was those early years the family spent traveling across the Southwest, but Kevin decided early on what his future profession would be—a cowboy, or if that fell through, an astronaut. He and Joseph often pretended to be cowboys in the Old West or astronauts and aliens flying through space. Joe was happy to indulge his older brother's ambitious fantasies, but he wanted to be a comedian one day. He was a silly, goofy child who was full of energy and loved telling jokes. The pair certainly kept their parents on their toes!

With two young children to think of, Paul and Denise decided to settle down for a little while. Paul was offered a job as the worship leader at Christ For the

Nations Music in Dallas, Texas, so the family packed up their bags and set off for the Lone Star state. Christ For the Nations Institute is a ministry training school founded in 1970. More than 28,000 students have graduated from the institute and gone on to dedicate their lives to evangelical work. Paul led worship services, taught music students at the institute, and worked on his own music. While at CNI, Paul honed his writing skills, penning several songs that became popular in churches across the country, including "Come as a Mighty River."

The little Jonases adjusted quickly to life in Texas. They spent a lot of time running around Christ For the Nations and listening in on their parents' music projects. Kevin and Joe were probably very inspired by all of this early musical influence, even if they didn't know it yet! Shortly after the family moved to Dallas, they got some exciting news. Denise announced that she was pregnant again. Nine months later, on September 16, 1992, Nicholas Jerry Jonas was born.

Nick had a distinctive personality right from the start. As soon as he could talk, Nick began singing, and he was a natural-born performer. When he was only two years old, he used his grandmother's turkey baster as a microphone, and her coffee table as a stage for his performances. When his grandmother tried to get Nick down off the table, he replied, "No, I need to practice. I'm going to be on Broadway." When he wasn't honing his performance skills, quiet, shy Nick loved to tag along after his older brothers. The Jonas boys, like all brothers, had fights over silly little things like toys and chores, but for the most part they loved spending time together.

After several years in Texas, Denise and Paul were homesick for the Northeast. In 1996, the family moved to Wyckoff, New Jersey. Most kids would have been heartbroken to be torn away from their school and friends, but not the Jonas boys. "I only really had one big transition and that was in third grade. I went from Dallas to New Jersey. Other than that I only switched schools after middle school and going to high school. So it was never really that big of a deal to me," Kevin explained to *Cross Rhythms*.

The Jonas boys flourished in New Jersey. Wyckoff is about twenty-five miles outside of New York City, so the move opened up a world of culture to the young children. The family took many trips into Manhattan to visit the American Museum of Natural History, see Broadway shows, and play in Central Park. Nick was especially inspired by New York City's theater scene. *Peter Pan* was his favorite musical in those days. He even had a performance of it on DVD. "I watched *Peter Pan* five times a day," he told *Clubhouse*. "I would watch every single movement—the dancing, how they acted, how their mouths moved when they sang."

The brothers were enrolled in Eastern Christian School, a private pre-K–12 preparatory school. The small classes and dedication to Christian values appealed to Paul and Denise. Kevin was in third grade, Joseph was in second grade, and Nick was starting kindergarten.

Kevin, Nick, and Joseph had a lot of fun growing up in New Jersey. They loved swimming and riding their bikes, and their proud parents took plenty of pictures of their boys! The brothers also enjoyed all the things that most young boys enjoy, like sports, video games, reading books, and watching cartoons. Some of their favorite cartoons were *Veggie Tales* and Nickelodeon's *Blue's Clues*. Joseph even dressed up as Blue from *Blue's Clues* and Nick as Bob from *Veggie Tales* for Halloween one year (Kevin went as Cavity Sam from the Milton Bradley game Operation)! Their other favorite shows were Nickelodeon's *All That* and anything on the Disney Channel, so they must have been pretty excited when they later formed a partnership with Disney. Kevin, Nick, and Joe have always cracked each other up playing silly games, making jokes, putting on comedy and music shows for their parents, and making goofy home videos.

Denise and Paul were also adamant that music continue to be a part of their boys' lives. The brothers learned to play piano, and the family often had sing-alongs around the piano in the evenings. Kevin taught himself how to play guitar when he was eleven years old. He was home sick from school one day. He picked up one of his dad's guitars, found a book on guitar basics, and spent the rest of the day learning the main chords. He even pretended to be sick for another two days so he could stay home and play! Quiet Kevin is a bit of a perfectionist and was soon playing like an expert. He taught both of his brothers how to play, although Joseph picked it up better than Nick. Nick learned how to play drums and is a piano wiz.

The Jonas boys also spent a lot of time at church. Religion had always been a big part of the brothers' lives, but as they grew older, they each made personal decisions to be Christians. Paul was offered a position as a senior pastor at the Wyckoff Assembly of God, a local evangelical church. He worked tirelessly to build up the church's outreach and music programs, and continued to travel to other congregations to aid with their worship programs. He also kept writing and performing music. Denise kept busy working with the hearing impaired as well as helping her husband at the church and keeping tabs on her three active boys.

The Assembly of God became a home away from home for the Jonas family. Kevin, Nick, and Joe were very involved in outreach programs, Bible studies, and worship services. As soon as Nick was old enough, he joined the church's children's choir—he even sang with the adult choir a few times! His poignant, soulful voice got everyone's attention. Nick loved performing so much that when he was only six years old, he started a drama group called the Radicals at church. He and his friends would put on skits based on Bible stories for the younger kids. The Radicals are still active at the Assembly of God and perform six outreach programs a year.

The brothers were very proud of their parents' work, as Nick explained to *Cross Rhythms*: "They started a sign language ministry. They went all over the world. It was pretty amazing. They stopped when I was born, which was thirteen years ago. Then my dad became the senior pastor at the church in Wyckoff, New Jersey, when we moved there. It was just amazing how the Lord planned it all. We moved to New Jersey and right there is where everything happens in the music industry and it kind of all came into place. It was really cool."

The Jonas family was very happy in New Jersey. Paul and Denise's work was going well, and the boys were excelling at their new school. Little did they know that stardom was waiting right around the corner, and it all started with a haircut . . .

CHAPTER 2
GIVE NICK'S REGARDS TO BROADWAY

Nothing made Nick happier than singing. He sang everywhere—in the shower, on the street, and even at the local barbershop. His mother took six-year-old Nick to the local barber to get his curls trimmed, and he entertained everyone in the shop by belting out some of his favorite show tunes. But what Nick didn't know was that one of the women in the shop was friends with an influential talent agent in Manhattan named Shirley Grant. She was so impressed with little Nick and his big voice that she gave Shirley's card to Denise and urged her to call the talent agent.

For days, Nick begged his mother to let him meet the talent agent—he had been dreaming about starring on Broadway since he was two, after all. Nicholas was easily the most ambitious of the young Jonas boys. While his brothers were enjoying school and playing sports, Nick had one goal and one goal only—he wanted to be famous. His parents finally relented, and Paul and Denise took Nick to the Shirley Grant Management offices in Manhattan to audition for Shirley. Most six-year-olds would have been nervous to perform for a total stranger, especially with such a big dream on the line, but not Nick! He was always a little shy when meeting new people, but as soon as he started singing, all of his shyness melted away. After singing a few songs for Shirley, she could tell he was a born performer. Shirley offered to represent Nick, and the Jonases accepted. Nick was on his way to becoming a star!

Nick must have been super-excited to be one step closer to achieving his dream. He already had plenty of practice belting out tunes in his living room. "From the time I was two years old, I would wake up in the morning and start singing all the time, every second of the day," Nick told MusicRemedy.com. But Nick probably had to spend a lot of time practicing songs and monologues for his auditions. When he felt ready, Shirley sent him on auditions for plays and musicals on and off Broadway, commercials, and recordings. Nicholas wanted to succeed at every audition, but he was especially determined to land a role on Broadway. "From whenever I can remember, I've been telling my grandma I was going to be on Broadway," he told *TeenStar*. Most casting agents had probably never seen a child with such ambition—especially not one so young!

Nick immediately began landing roles. He sang backup vocals on several recordings, had bit parts in a few commercials, and performed in a number of off-Broadway productions in New Jersey and New York. Kevin and Joseph got in on the act, too. They signed on with Shirley as well and landed roles over the next six years as extras alongside their youngest brother in commercials for Clorox, Burger King, Legos, Chuck E. Cheese, Battlebots, and the Disney Channel, just to name a few. Little did the Jonas brothers know that their early work with the Disney Channel was just the beginning of a long partnership, but more on that later! The boys must have loved being on set together, especially while filming toy and food commercials. After all, who wouldn't love to get paid to play with cool toys and eat delicious burgers and pizza?

Nick was seven when he took his first step toward the bright lights of Broadway. He was chosen to play the roles of Tiny Tim and Young Scrooge in *A Christmas Carol: The Musical* at Madison Square Garden. *A Christmas Carol: The Musical* was the first Broadway-style production to be staged at the WaMu Theater in Madison Square Garden. It ran from 1994 until 2004 and was choreographed and directed by Tony Award winner Susan Stroman. In those ten years, over 2.5 million people saw the show. Nick was a part of the cast for the 1999 holiday season.

Nicholas landed one of the most famous roles in *A Christmas Carol: The Musical*. He played the part of Tiny Tim, the crippled young son of Scrooge's clerk,

Bob Cratchit. Tiny Tim is sick and crippled, but he is cheerful, hopeful, and full of faith. It is Tiny Tim's plight that really makes Scrooge see how wrong his penny-pinching, greedy ways were. It was a lot of responsibility for Nick to take on such a pivotal role. He even had the responsibility of uttering one of the most famous lines in the entire play, "God bless us, every one." Nick wasn't a bit nervous—okay, maybe just a bit—but he was extremely excited. In addition to Tiny Tim, Nick played Young Scrooge in several scenes when the Ghost of Christmas Past visits Scrooge. Playing dual roles certainly kept Nick hopping backstage, but he loved every minute of it. Nick was born to perform, and live performances have always been Nick's favorites. His big voice filled the theater night after night as he belted out classic Christmas carols and wowed audiences with his standout performance. Nick was busy every minute of that holiday season, but a lead role in one of the biggest shows in Manhattan was the best Christmas present he could ever have asked for.

Nick caught the eye of several Broadway heavyweights during his run in *A Christmas Carol,* and in 2001 he landed his first role on Broadway. Nick won the part of Little Jake in Irving Berlin's *Annie Get Your Gun* opposite Crystal Bernard and country music star Reba McEntire.

Nick's big moment in the musical occurred when his character sang "Doin' What Comes Natur'lly" with Annie. Little Nick looked adorable dressed in a brown leather jacket and pants and a coonskin cap. His booming voice and ability to quickly pick up choreography really set him apart from the other child actors. Working with established stars like Reba McEntire and Crystal Bernard must have set a great example for Nick that would come in handy in his next role, as the adorable little teacup Chip in *Beauty and the Beast.*

Nick was nine years old when he joined the cast of *Beauty and the Beast* on Broadway. He performed as Chip every Wednesday evening, Friday evening, Saturday afternoon, and Sunday evening for six months.

The musical follows the story of Belle, a beautiful and intelligent French girl, and the Beast, a cursed prince. Belle is imprisoned in the Beast's castle. While there, Belle discovers that all of the household objects are alive, the victims of a cruel enchantment.

Chip, the part Nick played, is the adorable teacup son of Mrs. Potts, the head housekeeper, who was transformed into a teapot. The role called for a young actor with a resounding tenor voice, great comedic timing, and a lovable smile—naturally, Nick was a perfect fit. It was a much bigger role than his part in *Annie Get Your Gun*, and Nick was very excited for the chance to really show off his acting chops. His vocals were featured in the songs "Be Our Guest," "Human Again," "The Battle," and the reprise of "Beauty and the Beast." He also got to wear a fun teacup costume that fitted down over his shoulders and ride around in a special cart for portions of the play. Nick loved playing Chip and was very excited when the producers wanted him to sign on for another six months, but fate stepped in and intervened before he could sign a new contract.

Nick hadn't been certain he would be asked to extend his run with *Beauty and the Beast,* so he had continued auditioning for other shows. A few weeks before he was going to sign his new *Beauty and the Beast* contract, he got some incredible news. He was invited to join the Tony Award–winning cast of *Les Misérables* in the role of Gavroche. "I was at Bible camp," Nick told *Clubhouse*, "and I felt God saying, 'You're going to be in *Les Misérables* and touch many people.'" Nick happily accepted the role and joined the final cast of *Les Misérables*.

Les Misérables, or "Les Mis," as fans affectionately call it, is an emotionally charged musical set in Paris during the French Revolution. It is an adaptation of Victor Hugo's 1862 novel of the same name.

The role of Gavroche is a pivotal one in *Les Misérables*, and it was the biggest role Nicholas had ever played. He had many lines, a solo song, and a dramatic death scene, but he was ready for the challenge. The messages of redemption, hope, and love that form the foundation of *Les Misérables* were all messages that Nick believed in. He worked harder than he had ever worked for a show and wowed critics with his performance. Being a principal member of a Broadway cast has its advantages, and Nick was proud to be part of such a distinguished community. "It's awesome; I love everything about it," Nick told *Clubhouse*. "It's so exciting to go onstage every day—to sing a song and know 1,500 people are watching!"

Nicholas wasn't the only Broadway baby in the family. Joseph had appeared in several commercials with Nick, but he had never had any desire to sing or act. He was set on becoming a comedian, until one day he tagged along with Nick on one of his auditions. Nicholas was auditioning for a role in the musical *Oliver*, and the producers were very impressed with his look, amazing voice, and professionalism. They jokingly asked if he had any brothers, and Nick answered very seriously that he did, in fact, have a brother named

Joseph who was waiting out in the hall. The producers asked Joe to come in. They liked his look as well and asked him to return the next day for his own audition. "I didn't know what to expect," Joseph told the *Kansas City Star*. "I went home and learned the song that night and I was like I'm not going to sing! I already have my guitar." Unfortunately, neither Joseph nor Nick was cast in *Oliver*, but Joseph did eventually land a role in a Broadway show that was right up his alley—Baz Luhrmann's *La Bohème*.

La Bohème ran from December 8, 2002, through June 29, 2003, at the Broadway Theatre. Baz Luhrmann is the critically acclaimed director of the films *Romeo + Juliet* and *Moulin Rouge*. When he decided to bring Puccini's classic opera *La Bohème* to Broadway, the theater world took notice. He decided to relocate the story from 1840s Paris to the bohemian Left Bank of Paris in 1957. The opera was performed exactly as it was scored in the original Italian, but subtitles helped the audience follow the plot.

Luhrmann billed *La Bohème* as "the greatest love story ever sung." Giacomo Puccini originally wrote it in 1896. It is the story of several poor artists living in Paris, and their struggles to find love and overcome poverty and disease.

La Bohème is a tragic love story that has resonated with people from all walks of life since its debut. It has been performed in almost every opera house in the world and has been adapted again and again to appeal to new generations. The most famous adaptation is the Tony Award–winning Broadway musical *Rent*, which sets the story in the East Village of New York City in the 1990s. Joseph must have been honored and excited to be a part of *La Bohème*'s rich history. He performed with the children's chorus and learned a lot about showmanship from Baz Luhrmann. "That was pretty amazing. It was a great experience. I think it was really preparing me for what I'm doing today. You know, discipline and all that stuff that's needed for what you're doing in the music industry. I loved the experience," Joe told *Cross*

Rhythms. The show was nominated for seven Tony Awards during its run. With a show like that under his belt, Joseph was well on his way to being as in demand on Broadway as his brother Nick. But as luck would have it, neither of them would have time to commit to another Broadway show—they would be far too busy catering to a different type of audience.

CHAPTER 3

THE FAMILY THAT PLAYS TOGETHER STAYS TOGETHER

With Nicholas and Joseph performing on Broadway, things got pretty busy at the Jonas household. Denise began homeschooling all three of the boys so that they would have more time to pursue their dreams. It also meant that the family had more time to spend together, which was good because the family was growing.

On September 28, 2000, Frankie Nathaniel Jonas was born. Little Frankie was a very welcome addition to the Jonas household. The boys must have been very excited to have a new little brother to play with, and Frankie has always wanted to be just like his older brothers, which means that someday Frankie might be rocking out onstage, too! As Frankie grew up, he earned the nickname "Frank the Tank," although fans sometimes refer to him as the "Bonus Jonas." Frankie is the boss according to his brothers, and he always gets his way. With his impish smile and head of dark curls, there's a good chance Frankie will grow up to be just as cute as Kevin, Joe, and Nick.

With a new little brother, a successful Broadway career, and a loving family, Nick had a lot to be thankful for, but he knew that there were many other kids who weren't as lucky. During the winter of 2002, Nick was performing in New York City. Every day as he walked to and from the theater with his dad, he saw homeless kids and families huddled in doorways or crouched on park benches. It broke Nicholas's heart to see so many children suffering in a city where people were paying hundreds of dollars a night just to see him sing. He also knew that there were countless other children suffering that he had never seen or heard of, and he wanted to help them all. Nick didn't just want to donate money or volunteer; he wanted to create a charity especially for New York City's children in need. With his family's help and the support of his church, Nick founded the Nicholas Jonas Change for the Children Foundation. The nonprofit organization was devoted to the needs of homeless, abused, and terminally ill children in the greater New York area. Nick really wanted it to be a charity that helped children through the effort of other children. He rallied the support of his brothers, friends from church and school, and many of the other child actors on Broadway to help raise money and volunteer their time to make a difference in their communities.

The foundation has since shut down, due to lack of community interest. When Nick's career really took off, he didn't have the time to personally drum up support, and without his tireless devotion, not many people donated money. But Nick hasn't given up on this dream, so keep on the lookout—there's sure to be another Nicholas Jonas foundation in the future! Nick remains very devoted to charitable causes and helping those less fortunate than himself; he just has to go about it in a different way now.

You wouldn't think that Nick would need any more hobbies. He had a steady gig on Broadway, a charitable organization to run, church, schoolwork, and friends, but Nick felt that something was missing. In 2003, several Broadway artists were asked to record classic Christmas songs for the annual Broadway Equity Fights AIDS CD, a compilation album to benefit AIDS research titled *Broadway's Greatest Gifts: Carols for a Cure, Vol. 4.* But none of the classic Christmas songs seemed like a good fit to Nick. He was feeling inspired by the spirit of the Christmas season and deeply touched by the plight of those less fortunate, and he wanted to sing something that reflected his feelings. Nick turned to his father, who, after all, had been a musician for years, and the two of them set about writing a song. Nick had definitely inherited his father's ear for music, and a song quickly took shape. They named the song "Joy to the World (A Christmas Prayer)," and the lyrics were an emotional plea for peace and compassion during Christmas and all year long. With his song, Nick reached out to children who were starving, suffering, or alone, and hoped that listeners would feel compelled to get involved in their own communities after hearing it. "Joy to the World (A Christmas Prayer)" tackled some very adult issues, but Nick was wise beyond his eleven years and he knew that they were issues that needed to be addressed. Nicholas's dad recognized that they had created something truly special, so in November 2003, he sent a demo recording of Nick singing his song to INO Records, a Christian record label. INO is the record label of several big names in Christian music, like MercyMe, Caedmon's Call, and Chris Rice.

The executives at INO were blown away by Nick's emotional voice, mature demeanor, and stage presence. They sent the song out to every Christian radio station across the country and the song was put into heavy rotation. Nick's song struck a chord with listeners, and within two weeks, it was the most added and most increased airplay song on the Hot Christian Adult

Contemporary chart. "Joy to the World (A Christmas Prayer)" was, by far, one of the most popular Christmas songs that year. It was re-released on October 3, 2006, on *Joy to the World: The Ultimate Christmas Collection*, a compilation of Christmas music from INO.

Nick must have been pretty proud of himself. After all, not everyone has a hit song on the first try! But Nick was still surprised when INO Records offered him a recording contract. INO had never signed such a young artist before, and they knew they were taking a big risk. According to Jeff Moseley, president of INO Records, "I entered into the idea of working with a twelve-year-old with fear and in trepidation. My fears have quickly resolved after realizing just how purposeful he is about what God has called him to do. He has an amazing sense of acuity when it comes to goals and dreams. In today's age with pre-manufactured pop, even as young as he is, Nicholas is a breath of fresh air as he has the ability to 'voice' his projects through his singing and songwriting."

Nick worked on his album all through 2004, and that September, he was offered a very special opportunity. Nick was invited to sing "Joy to the World (A Christmas Prayer)" for the delegates at the United Nations to commemorate those who had lost their lives on September 11, 2001, when the Twin Towers fell. Nick took the responsibility seriously and delivered a moving rendition of his song. The events of September 11, 2001, had a huge impact on the Jonas family. Living so close to New York City, they witnessed the destruction and needless loss of life firsthand. Nick was especially heartbroken by the thought of the children who had lost parents. He felt very honored to be able to commemorate their deaths in front of such an influential audience.

Nick decided to call his debut album *Dear God*, and he wrote music for it with his dad and his brothers. Kevin and Joseph helped Nick write eight out of the eleven proposed songs for his CD. Not wanting to be left out, four-year-old brother Frankie tried to get in on the action, too. "He's doomed," Nick told *Clubhouse* with a laugh. "He sat down at the piano and said, 'I'm writing a song.'" The boys drew inspiration from their own lives, and they wrote anytime and anywhere the inspiration struck. They even wrote one of the songs, "Time for Me to Fly," in the car on the way home from a Michael W. Smith concert! Each of the boys brought something different to the songwriting, and the results were astonishing. Serious Kevin was brilliant at finding the perfect lyrics when everyone else was stumped, and his guitar riffs gave the songs their catchy edge. Goofy Joseph was great at adding in the fun, clever lyrics that would make the group popular later on, and Nick brought soulful vocals and topics for inspirational tunes. Paul, the boys' father, helped his sons mix everything together to produce songs with a young but polished feel. Nick couldn't have been more excited about the opportunity to share his music with the world. "This is my first record, so I'm very excited about this new experience and I am so blessed to have a family that is so loving and supportive of what I'm doing," Nick told About.com. "I hope this record touches a lot of people . . . The hope of this record is to make people feel good and happy inside. I'm excited to see what comes next."

In early 2005, Steve Greenberg, the incoming president of Columbia Records, heard a demo of Nick's album. He didn't really like the album, but he was impressed with Nick. He invited Nick to give a showcase for the bigwigs at Columbia Records. Nick took the stage with Kevin and Joseph playing guitar and singing backup vocals. They played one of the songs they'd written together, "Please Be Mine." While watching the boys play together, something clicked for the folks at Columbia. As Steve Greenberg explained to Reuters.com, "I liked the idea of putting together this little garage-rock band and making a record that nodded to the Ramones and '70s punk." Nick as a Christian solo act would be great—but Nick plus his brothers as a secular group would be phenomenal. They asked Nick, Kevin, and Joseph if they would be interested in recording an album as a band, and the boys accepted immediately. Nick told *Time for Kids* that he wasn't the least bit sad about losing out on a solo deal: "We are not competitive in our career. In our career we are very supportive of each other." Recording with his brothers would be three times as much fun, and recording primarily secular music would allow the brothers to access a much wider fan base.

They were on their way, but the brothers still had a lot of work to do before they could really call themselves a band. They needed to head into the studio with a new team of writers and producers to define their sound, write some songs, and, of course, come up with a name for their newly formed trio. If anyone was up for the challenge, it was Kevin, Joe, and Nick!

CHAPTER 4
IT'S ABOUT TIME

With the green light from the folks at Columbia Records, Kevin, Nick, and Joe were well on their way to becoming the band we all know and love. But first, they had to record some songs. Columbia paired the new trio with some of the best songwriters and producers in the business to help the boys write some serious hits. The brothers would have preferred to write all of their own songs, but they knew they still had plenty to learn and gladly accepted the help.

Some of the writers that they worked with included Adam Schlesinger (Fountains of Wayne), Michael Mangini (Joss Stone), Desmond Child (Aerosmith, Bon Jovi), Billy Mann (Jessica Simpson, Destiny's Child) and Steve Greenberg (Joss Stone, Hanson). Greenberg and

Mangini are the Grammy Award–winning duo behind Joss Stone's two critically acclaimed albums. They produced the Jonases' first album and drew heavily on the cheesy upbeat sounds of 1970s British punk rock and the grungy edge of garage rock. The result is "music on Red Bull," as Kevin puts it.

"We actually wrote seven out of the eleven songs. We're really happy about the songs we got to write on the album, and we love the songs we didn't write," Joseph explained to ym.com. Kevin agreed. "A bunch of other artists worked on our record, which is really cool; we got to work with some really great people."

The boys made demo recordings of over sixty songs for the album, and Joseph claims they wrote over a hundred. So where did they get all the subject matter for over a hundred songs? Their lives and personal experiences, of course! The boys always strive to write songs about subjects and experiences that really matter to them. Nick explained it best to ym.com. "We don't sit there and think about what people want to hear; we just write about something because we want to, like when we wrote the song 'Mandy,' we knew we needed an upbeat song for the record, but we didn't think about [what's going to be popular], we just wrote it, because it was important to us."

Each boy chooses subject matter for songs differently. "For all of us, it's different things," Kevin told the *Montclair Times*. "Girlfriends, the family around us, people we've known . . ." Most of the songs on their first album are about girls, and falling in and out of love. But no matter who comes up with the ideas the brothers work together to write their songs.

Kevin told ym.com that sometimes they can hammer out a song in under an hour, but other times they disagree: "We all work together, but that is something we fight about sometimes, not really anymore, but we went through that period about halfway through the album." Joseph would often get upset that none of the songs seemed quite right, or Nick would feel that Joe and Kevin were ganging up on him, like when the boys wrote their hit song "Mandy." Nick came up with the lyric "and all those boy bands," and Joseph and Kevin thought the line was stupid. Luckily, Nick won that fight. "Now it's the one line of the song the whole crowd sings," he bragged to ym.com.

The boys have a unique way of songwriting. Kevin explained the process to Scholastic.com: "We stand in a triangle and we will play with some chords on a guitar. Then we will go over it with some melodies. Nicholas will try, Joseph will try, then I will try, and we continue growing. We got really good at it." If you ask the brothers which one of them is the best at coming up with lyrics, they don't hesitate to answer. "Kevin has this ability, like we'll just put something in his ear and it'll come out of his mouth," Nick told ym.com. "Like it'll process properly out of his mouth and comes out perfectly with a rhyme scheme and everything," Joseph continued. But they all contribute pretty equally when it comes to writing their songs. Working with other writers was a new experience for the boys—they'd never written with anyone except each other and their father. The boys took all of the writers' advice to heart, and eventually they completed a number of songs they were pleased with.

It took over two years for the record company to be as satisfied. They kept pushing the album's release date back, hoping to find a few more singles they thought could top the charts. Columbia finally decided to have the brothers cover two songs by the British pop-punk band Busted. Busted is made up of three friends: Matt Jay, James Bourne, and Charlie Simpson. They sing upbeat pop songs with catchy choruses, and the trio is wildly popular in the United Kingdom. Columbia Records purchased the rights for two of their songs, "Year 3000" and "What I Go to School For." Kevin, Nick, and Joe had a great time recording the covers in the studio, and once the executives at Columbia heard them, they knew the album was finally ready. The finished album contained eleven songs:

"What I Go to School For"

"Time for Me to Fly"

"Year 3000"

"One Day at a Time"

"6 Minutes"

"Mandy"

"You Just Don't Know It"

"I Am What I Am"

"Underdog"

"7:05"

"Please Be Mine"

The boys decided to call the album *It's About Time*, since so many of the songs were related to the passage of time, including "Time for Me to Fly," "Year 3000," "6 Minutes," and "7:05." The title of the album was especially appropriate since it had taken so long to get the album into stores and the Jonas Brothers were getting tired of waiting—for them it was about time that their journey to stardom really began!

CHAPTER 5
POUNDING THE PAVEMENT

While Kevin, Joseph, and Nick were patiently awaiting the release of their first album, Columbia Records sent them on tour to start a fan base the old-fashioned way, through performing. The folks at Columbia knew that the boys had the performance chops to put them on the map with fans, and they didn't want to waste any time building buzz before the album dropped. Through most of 2005, the boys toured with some of the biggest names in music, including Kelly Clarkson, Jesse McCartney, the Backstreet Boys, and Click Five. "We started touring this past summer. Our first show was with Jesse McCartney, and we had so much fun. That was in July. It started then and has been nonstop until now. We have a blast on the road playing every night. We've been to forty-five of the fifty states of America. We're super-happy about that. My goal is to [tour] all of America in maybe two months," Nick told *Soundings Newspaper*. While on tour, they tried out different songs and different names, trying to figure out exactly who they wanted to be as a band. Turns out, it was simpler than they thought.

A band's name says a lot about them to their fans and potential fans, and Kevin, Joe, and Nick wanted to make sure they picked just the right name for themselves. It took the band quite a while to hit on a name that everyone was happy with. They considered names like "Jonas 3," "Sons of Jonas," and the "Jonas Trio" before they finally settled on the Jonas Brothers by accident. Nicholas told the story to *Cross Rhythms*: "We thought of many different names for the band, and the label was thinking of Jonas 3 at the time, and we didn't like that at all. So during the first show we did, we got onstage and said, 'Hey! We're the Jonas Brothers.' That's just who we were, you know? And that was our name from then on because that's how people knew us."

The boys had often toured with their parents from church to church, but they'd never been on a tour like this before. They were lucky if they managed to grab even six hours of sleep a night on their rickety bus! It was a lot of hard work honing their stage skills while on the road. "[Most people] don't understand how much work it really takes," Nicholas told the *Kansas City Star*. "You have to keep doing it every day, trying . . . building up your voice throughout the entire day, and then you have a show at like ten o'clock at night." Joseph agreed: "It gets tiring, but, you know, the fact of when you get back onstage, it's worth every bit. Every bit of energy that you spent to get there, it's completely worth it." They played a new town almost every day, and as the opening act for major stars, they had to make sure their performances were high-energy, fun, and up to the same standards as the veteran performers. "I'm pretty much stationary," Kevin told the *New Haven Register* about their performances, "just singing and playing my guitar. But Joseph and Nick, they run and do a ton. They jump around all over the place. Sometimes, if someone in the front row isn't paying attention, Joseph will run over and tap her on the shoulder and just start singing in her face. The first time he did that, the girl just started freaking out and loving it. It's a way to get everyone involved."

With such amazing performers to learn from, Kevin, Joe, and Nick worked hard and perfected their stage show. They were gaining fans in every town thanks to their brotherly chemistry, insane energy, and, of course, super-cute smiles. And as difficult as touring sometimes was, in the end, it was all worth it. "It's really let us do a grassroots thing," Kevin explained to the *New Haven Register*. "We've gone to different places and played and started a buzz. The reaction back home on the East Coast has been overwhelming. Every show we play, we run back to the hotel and check our MySpace page and we've got a bunch of friend requests. It shows people are liking what they see."

On top of practices, shows, writing new songs, and those oh-so-important six hours of sleep a night, the boys had schoolwork to do. After all, they still had to finish high school! Education is very important to the Jonases, so they started out every day on tour by getting their schoolwork finished, "because at night you're drained or in the middle of the day it's just like, you want to be able to focus and then that way you can do something fun. That's always good. We have hired tutors at home, but on the road, my work is like self-taught so I can teach it mostly to myself through the booklets," Nick told *Cross Rhythms*. Kevin has since graduated from high school, but Joseph and Nick are still working toward their diplomas and they take their studies pretty seriously. Cute and smart? Those Jonas boys are really special!

There were a lot of tour experiences that were really exciting for Kevin, Joe, and Nick. They loved getting to check out different towns and getting to hang out with other bands—especially bands that they really looked up to, like the Backstreet Boys. "It's crazy that one day I was singing Backstreet Boys songs in my basement—and just last week there I was onstage with them! Our dreams have really come true and we're so lucky," Nick said in a January 2006 press release from Columbia Records. It would have been easy to get caught up in the excitement of touring, but the boys always had family along for the ride to remind them of what was really important. "We keep it a very tight-knit group. Our father's our co-manager. Our road manager is our uncle. They're both pastors and they can both minister to us on the road. It's a really great thing to know that we have a tight and close group of people with us," Kevin explained to *Cross Rhythms*.

Toward the end of 2006, the Jonas Brothers signed on to do an Anti-Drug Tour with Aly & AJ and the Cheetah Girls. Both of those groups packed some serious girl power and had some serious girl fans, which was just fine with the Jonas Brothers. They love having girl fans! The Anti-Drug Tour went to schools across

America to educate kids about the dangers of drug and alcohol use. This was a very important tour to Kevin, Joe, and Nick because they strongly believe that no one needs drugs or alcohol in their lives in order to be happy or have fun. They would never do drugs, and they wouldn't want any of their fans to use drugs either. "We were totally for it, because we definitely want to make a difference," Joseph told the *Allentown Morning Call*. "We totally wanted to be a good influence." Getting the chance to share their feelings with their fans was an amazing opportunity for the boys. Most of the time, the bands would arrive at schools first thing in the morning. The bands and managers would talk to the students about drugs and alcohol and then the bands would perform. The performances were Joseph's favorite part, as he explained to the *Allentown Morning Call*: "It would be so funny because we would show up at the school, and it would be like seven o'clock in the morning. Kids would walk to school like, 'Oh, I want to go to bed'—totally super-tired, did not want to be in school that day. And we'd go, like, 'Okay, now here's the band,' and we would like totally rock out and the kids would go nuts."

The Jonas Brothers took a short break after a summer on the road and then opened for the Veronicas in early 2006. The Veronicas, a spunky twin sister act from Australia, were headlining their first tour to promote their album *The Secret Life of the Veronicas*, and the Jonas Brothers and October Fall were their two opening acts. "We're having a blast. We're going to schools every morning and playing shows with the Veronicas. Then we go to the venue for the night's show," Nick told *Soundings Newspaper*. Touring with a sister act was extra fun for the three brothers, and they got along well with all of the other performers. The boys had started singing some of the songs they'd written for their upcoming album, and they loved introducing their fans to their new music. "We've known for a while now how it felt to be onstage, but we never knew how it would feel to have people love music that we've written and that we both play and sing. It's very gratifying when fans come up to us after shows and tell us how much they relate to our songs," Joseph said in a January 2006 press release from Columbia Records. The boys were only on tour with the Veronicas for a few months, but it marked the end of almost a solid year of touring experience for the brothers. They had grown and matured a lot in that year and were more excited than ever to show the world just what they were capable of.

CHAPTER 6
MOVING ON UP

The Jonas Brothers were making headway with their touring, but they had yet to conquer the radio waves. Nick's "Joy to the World (A Christmas Prayer)" had been successful on adult contemporary and Christian radio stations, but the boys were hoping to break into the pop and Top 40 rotations. "With our music we're trying to be successful. It's definitely a pop record. It's a pop/rock record for the mainstream . . . We just feel like this is where we belong—this is who we are and let's just go for it," Kevin told *Cross Rhythms*.

But with their album still awaiting a release date, it was difficult to get airtime. Luckily, the boys took matters into their own hands and made sure the fans got plenty of their music by posting recordings and silly videos on their MySpace page. The fan response was overwhelming every time Columbia announced a new release date for the album. And Kevin, Joe, and Nick definitely appreciated the support. They were probably getting a little discouraged and anxious about their lack of a solid release date. After all, it had been almost a year since they signed their contract! But that holiday season, they got the best Christmas present they could have hoped for. Columbia decided to drop *It's About Time*'s first single, "Mandy," on December 27, 2005. The boys were absolutely thrilled with the news! "Mandy" was one of the songs Kevin, Joe, and Nick had written themselves and it was about one of their very close friends, so it was a special song for all of them.

Once "Mandy" hit the radio waves, girls across the country were wishing they were Mandy as they listened to the sweet and upbeat song the brothers had written about their friend. But one girl was smiling every time she heard it because she knew the song was about her—and who was she? Mandy, of course! Mandy was a childhood friend of all of the Jonas boys, but she was best friends with Nicholas when they were little. She and several of her friends were part of a sign language group that had taken lessons from Denise Jonas. "Mandy and two other girls are part of this group called Signs of Love. They play music, write songs, communicate in sign language, dance, and everything. They went to nationals for it and they ended up winning second in the nation for the sign language group. My mom works with them. She loves sign language," Kevin told Scholastic. com. As Mandy, Kevin, Nick, and Joe got older, it was Joe who became close with her. They dated for a while and remain friends to this day. The boys actually wrote "Mandy" while Joe and Mandy were dating. How's that for romantic? Any girl would love to have such a sweet song written about her, and Mandy was no exception. "Oh, she loves it! She is really cool," Joe told Scholastic.com. Of course she loves it; Joe really put his heart into the lyrics. He sings about how silly he can be but how Mandy always understands him and cares about him no matter what happens.

And the boys didn't just write a song about Mandy—they also asked her to star in the three music videos for the song! How lucky can one girl get? Even though Mandy and Joe were no longer dating by that point, they are still good friends and he wouldn't have wanted anyone else in the video with him! Shooting a video with one of their oldest friends was really fun for Kevin, Joe, and Nick. They could be themselves, goof off, and not have to worry about impressing her—which made all those hours of shooting fly by! The videos were directed by acclaimed documentary filmmaker Ondi Timoner, and they gave the boys the chance to show off their acting chops in a silly way. Timoner wanted to do something special for the Jonas Brothers' first music video, so he decided to shoot three videos to the same song! Each video would be for the song "Mandy," and each would tell one part of a longer story. The boys flew Mandy out to the set for their three-part video so that she could star as herself, but that's where the autobiographical part of the videos ends. Other than Mandy playing herself, the videos were purely fiction.

In the first video, Nick is watching Mandy in class. She drops her cell phone and he follows her, trying to return it. But when Nick catches up to her, Mandy's boyfriend, a popular jerk, starts bullying him. It cuts to Nick walking home alone. Suddenly a large SUV starts chasing him. It ends with, *To be continued . . .*

The second video picks up with Nick being chased by the large SUV. Inside are Mandy's boyfriend and his friends. Nick runs into the bushes to escape. Mandy's boyfriend and his friends get out and chase him on foot, but they can't find him. Nick has hopped into a car with Kevin and Joe. They pull into the street and drive off laughing. Later that night at the prom, Mandy and her boyfriend are crowned prom king and queen. Mandy seems happy, but when it's time for her to go home, her boyfriend doesn't want to leave. So Mandy goes out to the parking lot where the Jonas Brothers are hanging out. They drive Mandy home, but when they get there, her father is furious that she's late. He screams and hits her, and Mandy runs out of the house. She's about to jump back in the car with the Jonas Brothers when her boyfriend shows up. The video ends with Mandy trying to decide which car to get into.

The third video picks up the next day with Mandy sitting in the backseat of her boyfriend's car as he and his friends drive around smashing mailboxes. When they get to school, Mandy dumps him and walks over to where Nick and Joe are hanging out. But Mandy's now ex-boyfriend isn't letting her get away that easily. He comes over and starts bullying Joe and Nick. Mandy runs across campus and asks Kevin for help. Kevin and Mandy hop into his car and drive over to rescue Nick and Joe. Joe and Nick hop in the backseat, and they all drive away. The video ends with Mandy at the Jonas Brothers' concert, where the whole town (including Mandy's ex-boyfriend!) is there rockin' out.

The first of the three videos premiered on TRL on March 1, 2006. It stayed on the TRL top ten for weeks and peaked at number four. The second video for "Mandy" also made it onto TRL for a few weeks. And the third video premiered on TRL, but it never made it into the top ten. Seeing their music videos week after week on TRL was very exciting for Kevin, Joe, and Nick. Being featured on MTV is a huge step for any musician, since MTV only plays the hippest, hottest, most popular music and has the largest music fan base of any television channel in the country. With three videos for one song, the Jonas Brothers were getting a lot of exposure! "The coolest feeling was when we debuted our video on TRL. We went to TRL and going up to that window and seeing four hundred screaming girls, fans, I mean!" Joe, laughing, told *Cross Rhythms*.

Teenagers across the country were definitely sitting up and taking notice of the Jonas Brothers—and so were several music supervisors who were choosing music for hot new movies and compilation CDs. On May 17, 2005, a track from Nick's canceled solo album called "Crazy Kind of Crush on You" was featured on the *Darcy's Wild Life* sound track. *Darcy's Wild Life* was a television series on the Discovery Kids channel about a Hollywood actress and her daughter, Darcy, played by the beautiful Sara Paxton, who move from Los Angeles to the country. Darcy has to adjust to life on the farm without premieres, glitzy parties, and nonstop shopping. Nick was thrilled that "Crazy Kind of Crush on You" finally made it out there for fans to enjoy. One of the other singles from *It's About Time* called "Time for Me to Fly" was featured on the sound track for the film *Aquamarine*. And in March 2006, "Mandy" was featured on the Nickelodeon made-for-television movie special *Zoey 101: Spring Break-Up*, based on the hit Nick series *Zoey 101* starring Jamie Lynn Spears. The producers liked "Mandy" so much that they also put it on the *Zoey 101: Music Mix* sound track album.

The boys were flattered that their singles were receiving so much attention, but what they really wanted was for fans to have the chance to hear their entire album. They finally got their wish on August 8,

2006, when *It's About Time* was released. But the results were a little discouraging. It was a limited release of only 50,000 copies and Columbia wasn't doing much in the way of advertising and marketing to help album sales. But even with a limited release, *It's About Time* reached number ninety-one on the Billboard 200 chart, so there were fans listening. Columbia might have been losing faith in the Jonas Brothers, but the fans weren't, and neither were Kevin, Joseph, and Nicholas. They knew they had what it takes to be major music stars, and they weren't going to let anything hold them back.

The Jonas Brothers worked hard and did everything they could to get fans excited about their first album. Shortly after the album was released, their second single, "Year 3000," dropped. It was popular with fans and was getting a decent amount of airtime on pop radio stations. But what the boys never expected was how popular the song would become on Radio Disney. They were getting a tremendous amount of play, with tons of fans requesting more!

With all of that attention, Columbia decided to premiere the music video for "Year 3000" on the Disney Channel. The boys shot a super-cool video set in—when else?—the year 3000. They did most of the filming in front of a green screen. When the video was edited, the green screen was replaced with futuristic-looking buildings in an underwater dome! The special effects were pretty cool, but the boys' favorite part of the video shoot was the girls dressed up in silver outfits and pink wigs that they meet in the video. "We did some cool animation and graphic stuff, and all the girls have pink hair and [futuristic] outfits," Kevin told MTV.com. "It was fun to [shoot], 'cause when we got there, it was just really beautiful girls in futuristic costumes, and we were like, 'Ahhh,'" Joseph added.

Fans loved the "Year 3000" video, and album sales were holding steady, but Columbia just wasn't sure about the Jonas Brothers anymore. Columbia wanted the boys to go in a different direction with their music, but it wasn't a direction the boys were comfortable with. They wanted the boys to mimic other successful bands like Blink-182, but Kevin, Nick, and Joe didn't want to be anyone but themselves. On top of all of that, Columbia wasn't supporting the band with advertising, marketing, and publicity the way that the boys had hoped they would. In February 2007, the Jonas Brothers parted ways with Columbia. It was a mutual decision—Columbia didn't feel that the Jonas Brothers could sell enough albums, and the boys didn't feel that Columbia was providing them with enough opportunities. The Jonas Brothers had several successful tours and one fairly popular album under their belt, plus a huge fan base, but without a label they weren't going to get very far. They weren't ready to give up on their music yet, so a few weeks after leaving Columbia, the brothers started shopping for a new label. And this time they hit the jackpot. The boys were moving to Hollywood.

CHAPTER 7
WELCOME TO HOLLYWOOD

Most bands would have been devastated to lose their label's backing, but not the Jonas Brothers. They knew that bigger and better things were waiting for them, and they were determined to find them. So when Hollywood Records made the boys an offer, they jumped at the chance. Hollywood Records is the music arm of Disney, and it is the label of some of the hottest teen artists in the music business, like Aly & AJ, Hilary Duff, and the Cheetah Girls. Hollywood Records has a reputation for its nurturing family-oriented vibe and its ability to launch teen artists to super-stardom, and that was exactly what Kevin, Nick, and Joe were looking for. Hollywood Records and the rest of Disney were equally as excited to partner with the boys. "Kevin, Joe and Nick are the real deal—incredible musicians, phenomenal performers, charismatic stars," Gary Marsh, president of entertainment for the Disney Channel Worldwide, told E! Online. "An act like the Jonas Brothers doesn't come along very often. This is a giant coup for the Disney Channel."

Hollywood Records didn't waste any time putting their newest stars to work. The boys were excited to be working with new producers and were eager to get back into the studio—but this time they were doing it their way. As beneficial as it had been for them to work with seasoned songwriters on their previous album, they really wanted their sophomore effort to be their songs, their sound, and their chance to show their fans exactly what they had to offer. Luckily, Hollywood Records agreed. John Fields, who has worked with rock heavyweights like Rooney, Switchfoot, and Lifehouse, signed on to produce. Kevin, Joe, and Nick played him songs that they'd been working on since they recorded their first album, and he loved them.

"When we signed to Hollywood," Kevin told starpulse.com, "we told the label, 'Hey, we have some demos of songs we've been writing for the past year and a half.' We thought it'd be so funny to just record those songs for the album to see what we could get away with. But those turned out to be the songs on the record!" Fields, along with Paul Jonas, worked with the boys to polish their songs and decide which singles to feature, and then the boys went into the studio and laid down eleven new tracks in just twenty-one days! In addition to writing and singing all of the songs on the album, they played all the instruments. Kevin played lead guitar, Joe played guitar and keyboards, and Nick played keyboards, guitar, and drums.

Lots of artists spend months or even years recording an album, which just goes to show how seriously the Jonas Brothers take their music. "The album was very much a collaborative process," Kevin told *SingerUniverse Magazine*. "It's definitely our baby, but John completely understood our vision and made sure we were there to help him guide the process every day of the recording process. We rented out a house in Studio City that we called 'Rock House,' living there for the whole month of February and working from 11 A.M. to 11 P.M. in the attached facility called Underbelly Studios. It was a really awesome, one-of-a-kind experience."

They added two additional tracks to the album—"Kids of the Future," which they had recorded for the sound track for the Disney CGI film *Meet the Robinsons,* and "Year 3000," which was also on their first album. "Year 3000" was the most popular song with fans from *It's About Time,* and the brothers wanted to make sure that fans who hadn't been able to get their first album could have their favorite song. The final lineup for the album included:

"S.O.S."

"Hold On"

"Goodnight and Goodbye"

"That's Just the Way We Roll"

"Hello Beautiful"

"Still in Love with You"

"Australia"

"Games"

"When You Look Me in the Eyes"

"Inseparable"

"Just Friends"

"Hollywood"

"Year 3000"

"Kids of the Future"

Once the boys listened to the album in its final form, they knew immediately what to name it: *Jonas Brothers*. It was the first album that they had written entirely by themselves, and every song was personal—it was a true reflection of who they were, and they wanted their fans to know that immediately from the title. *Jonas Brothers* was released on August 7, 2007. It was the first album released with the new Disney-created CDVU+ (CD View Plus) technology. When the CD is played on a computer, it will give fans access to a special digital magazine that contains exclusive pictures, desktop wallpaper, buddy icons, and other interactive goodies that can be accessed on- and off-line.

The night of the release the boys celebrated on a cruise around New York City. Their parents rented a yacht and invited all of their friends and family to celebrate. Kevin, Joe, and Nick must have felt pretty blessed as they stood together on the deck of the boat, listening to their album and gazing out at the bright lights of Manhattan. Everything was finally falling into place—they finally had the right label and had just released a deeply personal album that they were truly proud of. What more could they ask for?

They may not have needed to ask for anything more, but they got it anyway! *Jonas Brothers* reached number five on the Billboard 200 chart within a week of the album's release. Their first single, "Hold On," and its music video had been released two weekends before the album dropped and were garnering major airtime—both on the radio and on the Disney

Channel and MTV. The music video for "Hold On," which featured the boys playing in a very windy room, reached number two on TRL. "S.O.S." was released as the album's second single within a few weeks of the album's release, and fans loved it, too!

Hollywood Records was determined to put the Jonas Brothers on the map as the hottest new band in the business, and the boys appreciated all of their efforts. "There's definitely a huge Top 40 plan in place for us by Hollywood Records with the new album," Kevin explained to *SingerUniverse Magazine*. "They have been incredibly supportive of our music as it's evolved and of our desire to reach as many fans as possible. Through them, we've had the opportunity to work with some amazing video directors like Declan Whitebloom, but they have allowed us input into the creative direction of each one. On the first album, we got to write seven of the eleven songs, but on the new one, we wrote or cowrote all twelve tracks!" Nick added, "When we did *It's About Time*, it was the first record we had ever done, and we have so much more experience to draw from now, both from doing so many live shows to spending all that time in the studio. We've had two more years now to become more proficient on our instruments and do all the things we needed to become a better band. We were a much bigger part of everything that happened this time."

As with *It's About Time*, the boys stuck to topics they knew when penning their catchy tunes. They wrote songs like "Hello Beautiful," "When You Look Me in the Eyes," and "Inseparable" about falling in love and songs like "S.O.S.," "Goodnight and Goodbye," and "Games" about the pitfalls of dating. They even threw in a few stirringly sad breakup songs, like "Still in Love with You," although it's hard to imagine anyone breaking up with one of the adorable Jonas boys! But perhaps the most telling song on the album is "Hollywood," which Kevin, Joe, and Nick wrote about leaving Columbia Records for Hollywood Records and their struggle to prove themselves all over again. The upbeat tune is a celebration of leaving a bad situation for a wonderful one and proving everyone wrong who doubted them. We're pretty sure that the folks at Columbia Records are kicking themselves now for letting the Jonas Brothers get away! But Kevin, Joe, and Nick don't have any hard feelings against their old label. They believe that everything happens for a reason, and they knew that the move to Hollywood had been the best decision they'd ever made, and things were only getting better and better every day.

CHAPTER 8

ON THE ROAD AGAIN

With their sophomore album in the can, Hollywood Records booked the brothers for public appearances and concerts and set them up on a summer tour. They performed for the president of the United States and his guests at the White House Easter Egg Roll in April. In August, the Jonas Brothers performed at Arthur Ashe Kids' Day at the USTA Billie Jean King National Tennis Center in Flushing, New York. Arthur Ashe Kids' Day is a day of tennis, music, and fun that benefits the United States Tennis Association's National Junior Tennis League.

The Jonas Brothers went back on the road in June and July 2007 for the Jonas Brothers Summer 2007 Prom Tour. They wanted to promote *Jonas*

Brothers before it released, and reconnect with their fans. But the boys also had an ulterior motive: They wanted the chance to experience a prom. Since Kevin, Joe, and Nick had switched to homeschooling so that they could pursue their music, they never got to attend a high school dance or prom. The Prom Tour was a huge success—after all, who wouldn't want to go to prom with the boys? The stage was set to look like a prom in a high school gym, and there were several photo booths set up in the crowd so that fans could get prom pictures made! "The tour has been amazing. It is one of my favorite tours so far. We have visited states from California to New York. We even went to Puerto Rico," Nick told *Time for Kids*. The Jonas Brothers have just one request for fans at their concerts—don't throw hard things at the stage! "I had lip gloss thrown at my guitar, my *brand-new* guitar . . . I was so mad," Nick complained to ym.com—so stick to soft gifts like stuffed animals and flowers, girls. It must have been really cool for the boys to go back to high school, so to speak, for a few months, but don't worry, they have no plans to trade in their life as a band for a regular high school existence!

Their summer tour was especially sweet because it was sponsored by one of the brothers' favorite candies—Baby Bottle Pops! Kevin, Joe, and Nick inked an endorsement deal with Baby Bottle Pops in conjunction with Nickelodeon in early 2007. The band remixed the Baby Bottle Pop jingle and recorded it in fifteen-, thirty-, and ninety-second versions. Then they filmed a fun commercial to go along with the jingles—it was a blast! The boys rocked out for a crowd of extras and everyone had plenty of Baby Bottle Pops to snack on! "Our mom and our little brother, Frankie, came out too so the whole family was out for the video shoot. It was really cool. They actually got to be a part of it so that was nice and we also played a couple songs for the extras in the commercial so that was cool, too. It was just an awesome experience. It should be airing now," Kevin told teenmag.com. Nickelodeon and Baby Bottle

Pops created a special website (www.bbpinvasion.com) where kids can access the Jonas Brothers' Baby Bottle Pops commercial, get special Jonas Brothers content like wallpaper and ringtones, and enter a sweepstakes to win a Jonas Brothers concert for their school. With Baby Bottle Pops sponsoring their tour, the brothers always had plenty of candy around, including extras of their favorite flavors. Joe loves strawberry, Nick likes watermelon and cotton candy, and Kevin's favorites are blue raspberry and watermelon.

The Jonas Brothers' second album, *Jonas Brothers*, was released as their Prom Tour drew to a close. The boys were itching to get back on the road and perform their new songs for their fans. So when they were invited to be a part of the hottest tour of the year—Miley Cyrus's Best of Both Worlds Tour—they immediately signed on.

Miley Cyrus is the bubbly actress and singer who plays Miley Stewart/Hannah Montana on the Disney Channel's hit series *Hannah Montana*.

When Hollywood Records decided to send Miley on tour, they knew that her opening act would have to be pretty sensational to keep up with her. Luckily they had the perfect band ready and waiting—the Jonas Brothers! The tour kicked off on October 18, 2007, and closed on January 9, 2008. They played fifty-four shows total, all of them completely sold-out. It was *the* tour of the year. Tickets sold out in most places within a few hours of going on sale, and scalpers were reselling tickets online for hundreds of dollars! Kevin, Joe, and Nick were touring veterans by that point, but nothing could have prepared them for the overwhelming response from their fans on that tour. Getting to play for sold-out crowds of dedicated fans was a dream come true for the brothers. Plus, the tour supported an amazing cause. One dollar for each ticket sold was donated to the City of Hope, a foundation that contributes to research for the prevention and cure of diseases that affect children around the world, like cancer. Giving back and rocking out? Nothing could be better than that as far as the

Jonas Brothers were concerned.

They were also pretty psyched to be touring with Miley. The boys had become good friends with the singing starlet before the tour, so traveling with her was a blast. "It'll be our first arena tour. We are so excited to be able to have the opportunity to tour with one of our really good friends," Nick told *Time for Kids* before the tour began. The only person who wasn't thrilled about the boys touring with Miley? Frankie Jonas—the littlest Jonas has a big crush on Miley, and he was jealous that his brothers got to hang out with her so much. "I actually had a problem with my *little* brother, Frankie. You know Miley Cyrus from *Hannah Montana*, right? Well, I was saying that I thought she was cute and he was like, 'What!' and ran over and started trying to beat me up," Nick explained to ym.com. Joseph added, "He has a picture of her on his wall with a heart around her face." Uh-oh, Nick, you better watch out! It sounds like Frankie is going to be quite the ladies' man someday.

JONAS BROTHERS

Nick, Kevin, and Joe show
off their star style

The brothers
at the 2007
Arthur Ashe
Kids' Day

Joe belting it out for his fans

Nick singing and strumming his acoustic guitar

Kevin rockin' a guitar solo

The Jonas Brothers love performing for their fans

CHAPTER 9

MEETING THE MOUSE

Since Hollywood Records is the music arm of Disney, the Jonas Brothers have enjoyed a close association with every section of the Disney empire. In addition to their record deal with Hollywood Records, the Jonas Brothers have joined forces with Disney for other projects. Even before they signed on with Hollywood Records, the big shots at Disney were impressed with the Jonas Brothers' talent and invited them to record some very special songs. For *DisneyMania 4*, the brothers did a cover of "Yo Ho (A Pirate's Life for Me)," a song made famous in the Pirates of the Caribbean ride at the Disney theme parks. The *DisneyMania* compilation albums always feature the hottest new stars performing their own versions of classic Disney songs, and it's a huge honor to be asked to contribute. The Jonas boys must have been thrilled to record "Yo Ho." All three of them love to ham it up when acting a part, so performing as pirates gave them plenty of opportunities to get in character. The finished recording was one of the highlights of the album. Disney was so impressed with the Jonas Brothers' energy, professionalism, and sound, that Disney asked them to record a new version of the theme song for their animated series *American Dragon: Jake Long*.

American Dragon is a cartoon about a Chinese-American boy named Jake living in New York City who discovers that he, along with everyone else on his mother's side of the family, can transform himself into a dragon. In his dragon form, Jake is bound to serve and protect the rest of the magical community, including leprechauns, fairies, mermaids, and other fictional beings, while avoiding capture from a group of warriors dedicated to killing all dragons. The cartoon's action-packed storylines and hilarious characters have made it a favorite with Disney Channel viewers. The Jonas Brothers' version of the theme song replaced the original version in the summer of 2006. The boys must have been really excited to hear their song kicking off such a popular show!

The Jonas Brothers were fast becoming fan favorites on Radio Disney, so when Disney planned a special tenth-anniversary celebration for their radio station, they just had to have the Jonas Brothers there. The boys performed along with other fan favorites like Aly & AJ, Miley Cyrus, the Cheetah Girls, and Bowling for Soup. "I think one of my favorite concerts so far has been the Radio Disney 10th Birthday show—that was an amazing night," Nick told Musicxcore. "It's kind of like an, 'Oh, let's play the best venue ever' kind of night," Kevin added. Radio Disney's Totally 10th Birthday Concert was held on July 22, 2006, at the Arrowhead Pond in Anaheim, California, and was broadcast live on Radio Disney.

After that thrilling concert, Kevin, Joe, and Nick

were excited to pair up with Disney again to record a cover of "Poor Unfortunate Souls" from the classic Disney Channel animated feature *The Little Mermaid*. Originally it was a slinky, subtly evil ballad, but the Jonas Brothers definitely put their own spin on it. They sped up the tempo and infused the lyrics with a gravelly urgency that gave the tune a more modern edge. The boys also filmed a music video for the song. They kept a water theme by filming at a community swimming pool where there were so many rules it was impossible to have fun. The Jonas Brothers show up and lead the kids hanging out at the pool in a mini-rebellion. Kevin, Joe, and Nick encourage the kids at the pool to break all of the rules, including jumping into the pool during adult swim! The video ends with everyone swimming and having a blast. Both the video and the Jonas Brothers' recording of "Poor Unfortunate Souls" were included on a two-disc special edition release of *The Little Mermaid* sound track in October 2006.

Once the Jonas Brothers officially signed on with

Hollywood Records in early 2007, they were put right to work. The first thing that Hollywood asked of their newest stars was to record a few more songs for sound tracks and compilation albums while they were waiting for the release of their sophomore album. So the boys went into the studio and pumped out several catchy, high-energy songs. On March 27, 2007, two albums were released simultaneously featuring the Jonas Brothers: *DisneyMania 5* and the *Meet the Robinsons* sound track. The boys recorded a cover of "I Wanna Be Like You" from the Disney animated film *The Jungle Book* for *DisneyMania 5*. They had a blast putting their own spin on one of their favorite songs from their childhood, and they gave it a definitively punk rock edge. The boys recorded a fun video for the song with a jungle theme. The video and song are featured on *The Jungle Book* Platinum Edition DVD, which was released in September 2007.

After monkeying around recording "I Wanna Be Like You," Kevin, Joseph, and Nicholas recorded a song for the sound track of *Meet the Robinsons,* a Disney CGI animated feature film about an orphan boy named Lewis who's searching for a family. The Jonas Brothers recorded a song called "Kids of the Future" for the sound track. It was a rewrite of Kim Wilde's "Kids in America." "Kids of the Future" is a positive, punk affirmation of the film's themes of love, acceptance, and family. The boys also filmed an amazingly cool video to go along with the song. The video scenes from *Meet the Robinsons* are intercut with the Jonas Brothers rocking out on a futuristic set. The video premiered on the Disney Channel and was played often, thanks in part to fan requests. *Meet the Robinsons* was a hit with families and kids and grossed over $152 million at the box office.

On August 25, 2007, the Jonas Brothers got their first real taste of life as Hollywood Record performers. They were the main attraction as they played for a screaming crowd at the closing ceremonies of the Disney Channel Games in Orlando, Florida. The Disney

Channel Games are a series of competitions that Disney puts on every summer. Stars from Disney Channel series and made-for-television movies are divided into teams and compete against each other in fun events like obstacle courses; extreme rock, paper, scissors; and super-soccer. The games take place over the course of the summer and are watched by millions of viewers, so the closing ceremonies are a big event. It was a fun concert for the boys, especially since many of their good friends were competing in the games!

The Disney Channel Games closing ceremonies concert was so popular with fans that the Disney Channel decided to have the Jonas Brothers headline a special televised concert in October 2007 called *The Jonas Brothers in Concert*. The brothers performed songs from *Jonas Brothers* and *It's About Time* for fans in New York City's Gramercy Park. The boys loved having the chance to rock in New York, especially since they grew up seeing concerts there!

For the 2007 holiday season, the Jonas Brothers

contributed a song called "Girl of My Dreams" to *A Disney Channel Holiday*, a compilation album of holiday songs by hip young bands and musical artists. The album also includes tunes by Corbin Bleu, Miley Cyrus, Ashley Tisdale, the Cheetah Girls, Billy Ray Cyrus, and KeKe Palmer.

The Jonas Brothers had conquered recording, making appearances, and putting on rockin' live shows, but they still had another area of entertainment that they wanted to break into—acting.

CHAPTER 10

I'M READY FOR MY CLOSE-UP

The Jonas Brothers had become fixtures on the Disney Channel, so the next logical step was to expand their television horizons. Nick and Joe already had plenty of acting experience thanks to their time on Broadway, and Kevin was a natural in front of the camera. The folks at the Disney Channel were keen to capitalize on the boys' acting skills and had some ideas for their new stars, including a guest spot on one of Disney's hottest shows, their own television series, and starring roles in a made-for-television movie.

The Jonas Brothers were thrilled to make the jump into acting and they were even more thrilled when Disney presented them with the idea for a series called *J.O.N.A.S.* The boys loved the concept and got right to work shooting the pilot. On the show, Kevin, Joe, and Nick star as three brothers in a band called the Jonas Brothers who tour the country with their father.

But the band is just a cover—the boys and their dad are really spies. In addition to being their last name, *J.O.N.A.S.* stands for "Junior Operatives Networking as Spies." They spend a lot of time trying to keep their spy jobs a secret from their mother, friends, and the media, especially a teenage reporter named Stella Malone. Their arch-nemesis is Dr. Harvey Fleischman, an evil dentist who wants to gain control over teenagers everywhere. "We went through a week and a half of martial arts training to get ready for it," reports Kevin to the *National Ledger.* "We had to do stunts. We were on cables and all that kind of stuff, and it was absolutely awesome. We actually trained with a guy named Koichi [Sakamoto]; he's the man who trained the Power Rangers, which was exciting for us." The guys were really pleased with the finished pilot and kept their fingers crossed that Disney executives would like it—

and they did! In October 2007, Disney announced that they were adding *J.O.N.A.S.* to the line-up for 2008. The brothers were ecstatic! They started filming after their tour with Miley Cyrus.

Before the boys ever went on tour with Miley, they became friends while filming a guest spot on her show, *Hannah Montana*. The episode, titled *Me and Mr. Jonas and Mr. Jonas and Mr. Jonas* aired on August 17, 2007, right after the premiere of *High School Musical 2*, the made-for-television movie sequel to the smash hit *High School Musical*. Over 10.7 million viewers tuned in to catch the Jonas Brothers in their television series debut. In the episode, the boys play themselves, so it wasn't too much of a challenge to get into character!

On the show, the Jonas Brothers meet Miley Stewart in her Hannah Montana disguise at a recording studio and hit it off—but not with Miley/Hannah. Instead the boys bond with Miley's dad, Robbie Ray (who is played by Miley's real-life dad, Billy Ray Cyrus). Robbie Ray writes all of Hannah's songs, and he agrees to write a song for the Jonas Brothers. As the boys bond with Robbie Ray through prank phone calls, silly games, and lots of horseplay, Miley becomes jealous. Miley and her best friend Lily, played by Emily Osment, dress up as two boys and convince the Jonas Brothers that they wrote the song Robbie Ray has been working on. Their plan almost works, but Robbie Ray manages to set things straight. He and Miley have a heart-to-heart and Robbie Ray decides the song would be best as a duet. At the end of the episode, Hannah and the Jonas Brothers perform the song "We Got the Party," which became an instant hit on the Disney Channel. "It's just a fun song; we love it. Actually some of the funniest parts of the show were when we were hanging out with the cast," Nick told Tommy2.Net.

Filming with the cast and crew of *Hannah Montana* was a great experience for the Jonas Brothers. They had a blast joking around and playing with the fun props from the episodes—including toy guns that shot foam balls. The boys helped Miley when she forgot lines during rehearsals, and Kevin coached Emily on "being a dude" for her scene dressed up like a boy. During breaks in rehearsals and shooting, the boys would entertain the crew by singing their favorite songs from the 1980s and dancing around. All of that goofiness and energy from rehearsals definitely helped when it was time to film—Kevin, Joe, and Nick gave an amazing performance that proved they had real acting chops.

The boys got the chance to give a different type of televised performance on August 24, 2007, when they performed two songs at the Miss Teen USA pageant. The boys played for the audience while the Miss Teen USA contestants paraded by in their evening gowns. The brothers had a lot of fun backstage chatting with the contestants and consoling the girls that didn't win. The contestants must have been just as excited to have the Jonas Brothers around as the boys were to be there—losing wouldn't be so bad with Kevin, Joe, and Nick there to cheer you up!

A few days later the band flew to Los Angeles to

present an award with Miley Cyrus at the 2007 Teen Choice Awards. They got dressed up in cool outfits and vintage sunglasses. "It's sunny out now so you gotta do the sunglasses," Nick told tigerbeat.com. "It's part of the look." Kevin was actually sporting a brand-new hairstyle for the event. His normally straight locks were even curlier than Nick's!

The 2007 Teen Choice Awards had a green, environmentally friendly theme and the red carpet was actually green. Once they made their way past the paparazzi, they were seated near Miley on a comfy couch and settled in to watch the show. The performers, including Avril Lavigne, Kelly Clarkson, and Akon, really pumped up the crowd, and lots of the presenters and award winners were hilarious. When it was their turn to present the award for Choice R&B Track, the boys took the stage along with Miley, who looked stunning in a sequined minidress. After listing the nominees, they announced that Sean Kingston was the winner for his hit single "Beautiful Girls."

It was a huge honor for the Jonas Brothers to be asked to present at the Teen Choice Awards show. Since teenagers across America vote to choose the winners, only the most popular young stars are asked to present— and that's why they asked the Jonas Brothers!

So what was next for Kevin, Nick, and Joe? They were headed off to summer camp, Jonas style. They flew to Toronto, Canada, to film the Disney original made-for-television movie *Camp Rock*. Kevin, Joe, and Nick star as the members of a band named Connect 3, who are celebrity counselors at a summer camp for aspiring musicians. *Camp Rock* will premiere on the Disney Channel in 2008. Disney has a well-deserved reputation for producing exciting television movies, so *Camp Rock* is sure to be a treat for fans! We can't wait!

CHAPTER 11
BEHIND THE MUSIC

The Jonas Brothers' journey to the top has certainly been a wild one! In just a few short years, the boys have gone from stage performers with small roles to rock superstars. The hectic schedules and busy days that come along with stardom are just fine with them, though, because they love what they're doing. But even with their busy careers, the boys still manage to have private lives.

So what do the boys do when they aren't performing? Well, like any teenage boys, they like to hang out with friends, flirt with girls, and just generally goof off. The boys love to roughhouse and can often be found wrestling, dancing around to loud music, or jumping on their beds and sofas. All that horseplay is a great way for the brothers to get out excess energy or to get pumped up before an event or show.

How else do they get pumped up before a show? "We actually have a forty-five-minute lockdown where no one leaves and no one comes in. We get ready for the show, we change, get focused, play through all of the songs from that night on the acoustic guitar, do vocals, pray, push-up, eat food," Kevin told Musicxcore. Getting pumped onstage is especially easy because the boys and their band have secret ways of communicating. "We give each other looks all the time where only we know what it means," Nick told *Bop*. "We could have an entire conversation with our band, and people will walk into our conversation and be like, 'What?'"

Kevin, Joe, and Nick spend a lot of time on their tour bus, and it's easy to get bored when stuck in such a small space for such long periods of time. Nick and Joe start their mornings off with schoolwork, then the boys will work on new songs, give phone interviews, and handle other business-related stuff. But once that is all done, they have free time—and that's when the brothers sometimes get into trouble! They have a small video camera and they love to make funny videos of themselves that they will post on their youtube.com or myspace.com pages. Sometimes the boys will record fake talk shows or do celebrity impressions, and other times they will just film each other doing day-to-day stuff but add in funny commentary. Joe and Nick both especially love making videos, and they really ham it up when they're on camera.

Another favorite way they fill their downtime is by making prank phone calls! Kevin, Joe, and Nick have been known to prank-call all their friends, management team, publicists, and even other stars, like Aly and AJ Michalka of Aly & AJ. The boys' prank calls are usually pretty funny, never mean. They'll pretend to be an angry parent whose daughter didn't win a Jonas Brothers contest or a fan desperate for info about the band. Luckily most of the people they prank-call are amused by the boys' antics!

The boys have made friends all over America while touring and they still have good friends in New Jersey from their childhood, but at the end of the day they are each other's best friends. Their bond is really strong, and working together has only made it stronger. "We just always have to remember that we're brothers before anything else. We're family." Kevin told Musicxcore. They do fight occasionally, but it's usually over silly stuff, and they always make up pretty quickly. "We're brothers and we are always going to have some quarrels. Nick always gets upset if I wear his socks. It is really funny," Joe told Scholastic.com during an interview. Kevin was quick to jump in, too: "We usually get along. We know we can't just get upset at each other and hold grudges against each other while we are onstage. It's not going to work." So what do they fight about? Clothes, lyrics when they are songwriting, and, of course, girls. "Because the girls we like are in between our ages," Kevin explained to ym.com. Luckily, not even a beautiful girl can come between these brothers for too long!

When Kevin, Joe, and Nick aren't on the road or working, they like to take time out at home in Wyckoff, New Jersey. They love their little house in Jersey, where Kevin and Joe share a bedroom, Frankie and Nick share a bedroom, and all four brothers share one bathroom! The boys do have a special recreation room where they all hang out with big comfy couches, a place for their musical instruments, and a big TV with an Xbox. Their mom makes them all of their favorite Italian meals when they're home, including pasta and lasagna. And just like in any other family, they have to help with the cleanup after dinner—their chores include taking out the trash, doing the dishes, and setting the table. They love getting the chance to catch up with old friends and just relax while home. "We like to play tennis, wiffle ball, hang out with friends when we have the chance, and go see movies," Nick told *Time for Kids*.

Another fun part about being home for the boys is the chance to visit the church where their dad used to be a pastor. Their faith is still a huge part of who they are, and it will always be important to them. Their favorite Bible verse is Matthew 5:14, "You are the light of the world. A city that is set on a hill cannot be hidden." Nick explained why the boys live by that verse to Musicxcore.com: "It's really important for us because it's like there's a lot of bad things that go on, but we gotta be the light . . . There's the band and there's all the success that comes with that, but in the midst of it all there's us being grounded and that's remembering where we're from." With that humble attitude, it's no surprise that the boys are on top. They don't take anything for granted. Lots of young stars get caught up in the trappings of fame and spend all of their time partying and posing for the paparazzi, but not the Jonas Brothers! They are dedicated to living a life based on their faith, which means they won't spend crazy nights in clubs, and they will never use drugs or alcohol. All three brothers wear promise rings on their left hands as reminders that they have pledged to remain pure until marriage. In addition to their personal moral convictions, the boys also have a strong support network of family and friends who help keep them grounded.

Even well-balanced, down-to-earth stars like the Jonas Brothers enjoy some of the perks of being famous. "People give us free clothes to wear, which is really cool . . . I haven't actually purchased any clothes in about a year," Nick told *Popstar!* The free swag and glamorous events are fun, but for Kevin, Joe, and Nick the best part of being in a band is their fans. Nick loves being recognized by fans when he goes out, as he told Musicxcore: "Uh, it's cool. To tell you the truth it's kind of exciting because it's like you're working really hard and all of a sudden people recognize all of your hard work. It's a cool thing." Kevin agrees: "We're never like, 'Oh hi'; we're always like, 'HEY!' and give them hugs and stuff. It's cool, you know . . . It makes our day." Fans write on the brothers' myspace.com page every day, leaving them encouragement and telling them how much they love their music.

The Jonas Brothers' fans are also really creative when it comes to getting the brothers' attention. They make amazing signs for concerts and give the brothers some really cool gifts. The boys say there are two gifts that have really stood out from the rest. The first is a model of the DeLorean, the time-traveling car from the *Back to the Future* movies. All three brothers love those movies, so the model was a great gift. The second gift that impressed the boys was a hippopotamus. Not a stuffed one or a figurine, but a real live hippo that lives on a wildlife preserve in Africa. The fan adopted the hippo, named it the Jonas Brothers, and then presented Kevin, Joe, and Nick with the certificate of adoption. "We were getting so many hippo gifts because we were doing that song 'I Want a Hippopotamus for Christmas.' We were getting, like, hippo pillows and, you know, hippos are the coolest things to get. But we looked and we were like, 'Oh cool, a picture of a hippo,' and they were like, 'No, that's your certificate, I got you a real hippo,'" Joe told Musicxcore. Now that's a creative gift!

Since the Jonas Brothers are always together, it's sometimes easy to forget that they are individuals with different likes and dislikes, but most fans have one brother that is their favorite! Girls who like the strong, silent type tend to be into Kevin the most. Kevin is the least flashy member of the band, but he's the glue that holds the band together, according to his brothers. He's very passionate and intense about music, and even if he wasn't in the band, he'd probably be pursuing music on his own. His Gibson Les Paul guitar is one of his most prized possessions, and he loves to just sit and play whenever he has something on his mind or when he needs a break from the world. "The moment I picked up a guitar, that was the minute I knew I wanted to do this for the rest of my life," Kevin told the *Kansas City Star*. He likes to start every day by watching music videos on MTV (so he can keep tabs on the competition!) and drinking a huge cup of coffee. He's worn glasses or contacts since he was little, and he can wear his dark hair straight or curly, although he prefers it straight.

Some little known facts about the oldest Jonas are that he is ticklish on his sides and that his favorite word is *excellent*—he even has his brothers saying it!

Kevin is slow to enter into relationships—he likes to make sure that a girl is right for him before he starts dating her. But once he has a girlfriend, he is very devoted. Kevin is much quieter than his brothers when it comes to his love life, but Kevin does have one big celebrity crush. "I'm in love with Ashley Tisdale," he told Tommy2.Net. Well, they both spend a lot of time at the Disney studios, so maybe Kevin will have a chance to work with his dream girl in the future.

When Nick wants to impress a girl, he has one fail-safe way of letting her know how he feels—he'll get his brothers to help him write her a song! "We'll put it out there pretty obviously," Kevin told *Bop*. Kevin's other trick for attracting girls? His car! He drives a "new Jeep Commander. Leather seats, black on black; only way to roll," he told Musicxcore. And once he scores a date with a special girl, Kevin has the perfect date all planned out, according to briomagazine.com: "We live in Wyckoff, New Jersey, so I believe the best date would be going to New York City and having dinner. A restaurant we like is La Mela. Tables are set up in the street covered with overhanging lights. Then head to a Broadway show." Kevin seems pretty mature and smooth, but he has had his share of embarrassing moments. "I've fallen off the stage before," Kevin told the *St. Petersburg Times*. "It had a catwalk-ish area and I didn't see that I was stepping out beyond it and I just kind of fell off the stage. I landed properly and then jumped back and tried to play it off like I meant to do it. But I definitely did not mean to do it."

Girls who love to laugh will usually claim Joseph as their favorite Jonas Brother since he has a reputation for being hilarious. It's a well-known fact that Joe wanted to be a comedian when he grew up, and he hasn't completely given up on that dream. He'd love to host *Saturday Night Live* someday and have the chance to participate in some of their famous comedy sketches. Joe gets teased a lot by his brothers for being the most concerned with his appearance. He takes the longest to get ready in the morning and is constantly borrowing his brothers' clothes, shampoo, moisturizer, and hair gel. "I take things from Kevin's closet, maybe a little from Nick," Joe laughingly told tigerbeat.com. He starts every day with a long run because staying in good shape is very important to Joe. Even when the boys are on tour, he'll find a way to get in his workouts. Joe is the only one of the brothers who really knows how to cook, and his specialty is breakfast. He's a wiz when it comes to preparing bacon, sausage, chocolate chip pancakes, and omelets, but his favorite breakfast food is Pop-Tarts. Joe doesn't usually get embarrassed. He loves to be in the spotlight—no matter what the reason—but he has had a few moments that made him blush. "One time I had a hole in my pants, like, the entire show and I didn't realize until, like, after the meet and greet and I got back and I sit down and I'm like, 'Oh man!' It was really embarrassing," Joseph told Musicxcore.

Joe is definitely girl crazy and very open about his romantic life. Right now Joe isn't looking for a serious relationship since he's been so busy with his career, but he has dated some high-profile girls in the past, including AJ of Aly & AJ and Mandy, who he made famous with the Jonas Brothers song "Mandy." Joe's ideal girl would be someone warm and funny who knows how to have a good time and who doesn't take life too seriously. If Joe was planning his ideal date, "It's all about the surprise. I like to have fun, so we'd go bowling," he told briomagazine.com. One of the best dates he ever went on was on Halloween. "I bought this huge costume to make my crush laugh," he told *TWIST* magazine. "I was dressed up as a cowboy riding a bull. I liked it because it had this button. When you pressed it, the cowboy suit blew up and became really huge! She dressed up as a milk shake. It was really, really awesome! We went trick-or-treating all day." So if you want to impress Joe, all you have to do is be easygoing and make him laugh.

The youngest Jonas, Nick, is the favorite of romantic girls everywhere. Nick has a reputation for being sweet, sensitive, and a hopeless romantic. Nick is quick to fall for girls, and many of the Jonas Brothers' songs are the result of Nick falling for a girl, as he told *Bop*. "When I really have inspiration for something, it's really easy for me to write a song." Girls definitely inspire Nick! He's been pretty quiet about his love life, but recently he's been linked to *Hannah Montana* star Miley Cyrus. "We've become very close," Nick told *TWIST* magazine about their relationship. In a separate *TWIST* magazine interview, Miley said, "I think we both are into each other, and there's definitely something there." Hmm . . . sounds like a romantic relationship might be brewing between those two! But if things don't work out with Miley, Nick will definitely be on the hunt for a special kind of girl. "She has to be kinda quiet, like a serious person—totally driven. People say I'm competitive, but I consider myself to be very driven," Nick told ym.com. He explained to briomagazine.com that if he was planning the perfect date, he "would buy box tickets to a Yankees' game [for him and his date] and watch the Yankees beat the Red Sox."

According to his brothers, Nick takes the longest to wake up in the mornings and starts every morning with a big breakfast and some quality time with his guitar. He prefers to write music in the mornings, when his mind is at its freshest. His favorite guitar is his red Gibson SG and his favorite Jonas Brothers song is "Please Be Mine" since it was the first song the boys ever wrote together—plus it's a soulful, romantic ballad and those are Nick's favorites! Some things about Nick that most fans might not know are that he is a neat freak when it comes to keeping his closet organized, he still wears a retainer at night, and he is ticklish right above his knees. Nick's most embarrassing moment on tour happened when he fell during a performance. "I fell onstage once . . . into our guitar player . . . I was kind of just like I better keep it down a bit because I was really rocking out and I just fell," Nick told Musicxcore.

But the one thing that really sets Nick apart from his brothers is that Nick has type 1 diabetes. Diabetes is an illness that affects how the body processes sugar. His body doesn't produce enough of the hormone insulin to convert sugar into energy. Nick was touring in November 2005 when he discovered he had the illness. He was thirsty all the time, was losing lots of weight, and was really cranky. Finally, his parents insisted that he see a doctor and the whole family was shocked to learn what had been going on with Nick. At first he was really frightened that he was going to die, but he bounced back quickly once the doctors explained what diabetes is and how it can be managed. Nick handles the disease bravely, as he told ym.com: "Most of the kids who find that they have diabetes go immediately into shock and are devastated . . . I looked at it that way for about five minutes, and then I was like, 'This is an opportunity.' I knew that I wanted to make an impact somehow, and this is just another step I can take and I hope that kids can see the positive influence that they can have on other kids as a result of this, even if it's not diabetes. Even if it's a small illness that you have for a day—I mean, Kevin learned how to play guitar because he was home sick from school for a day, so he took that and made an opportunity from it. This is an opportunity for me to be a better person . . . You have to pull yourself together and learn self-control and keep it cool. And I learn that every day."

Nick controls his diabetes with a wireless insulin system called OmniPod, which gives him ten or more shots of insulin a day to keep his body processing food correctly. Nick has inspired kids with diabetes across the country to not let their illness hold them back from chasing their dreams. His brothers are super-supportive, and all three of them are dedicated to raising money and awareness for diabetes research. What a way to make a difference!

CHAPTER 12
KIDS OF THE FUTURE

So what will the future hold for these hardworking, dedicated, and multi-talented brothers? The Jonas Brothers hope to release their third album in 2008 and continue touring. The band and their music will always be the Jonas Brothers' first priority when it comes to their career. But they do have some other projects that they would like to pursue. "We would like to get into TV, movies, anything. We want to conquer all of it," said Kevin in an interview with the Jonas Brothers Street Team. The boys are already filming the television series *J.O.N.A.S.* and the made-for-television movie *Camp Rock*, both of which will premiere on the Disney Channel in 2008. In addition to television, the boys want to act in some major motion pictures.

The boys have already recorded one duet with Miley Cyrus, "We've Got the Party," and it was so much fun that they would love to record duets with other artists as well. Kevin, Joe, and Nick are also looking forward to shooting more music videos. They love filming music videos with cool effects or a fun twist for fans to enjoy, like the video for "Hold On," which features wind so strong it almost blows them away!

In addition to their work as a group, each brother has separate dreams. They would all like to continue their education by attending college. Nick would like to return to Broadway—since it combines all of his favorite things: a live audience, singing, and acting! But when he does return to the stage, he'd like to take on more adult roles. Kevin would like to continue to pursue music and songwriting, and Joe has never completely given up on his dream of being a comedian.

No one can be certain exactly what the future holds, but the Jonas Brothers are here to stay.

CHAPTER 13

THE JONAS BROTHERS' PLAYLIST

The Jonas Brothers rock your world, but who rocks theirs? Their upbeat blend of pop, punk, and rock is totally irresistible. It's a mixture of a lot of different styles of music, but it's a mix that's all their own. To achieve that famous Jonas Brothers sound, the boys draw on all sorts of things that inspire them, including other musical artists they admire and respect. The brothers are always looking for new music—they even share one iTunes account! Each of the boys has different favorites, but there are a few musicians that have had a lot of influence on Kevin, Joe, Nick, and their music.

SWITCHFOOT

The Jonas Brothers list Switchfoot as their all-time favorite band. This Grammy-nominated alternative rock band is known for their energetic live shows and their soulful, probing lyrics. Their debut album, *The Beautiful Letdown*, was released in 2003 and sold over 2.6 million copies. The members of Switchfoot are all Christians, and, while their music is secular, they are very popular on the Christian music scene. They often headline shows at Christian music festivals and are very open about their faith. The Jonas Brothers share Switchfoot's attitude when it comes to balancing faith and their career—they want their music to reach everyone, but they don't hide the fact that they are Christians.

STEVIE WONDER

A lot of people have compared Nick to a young Stevie Wonder because of his sweet and soulful voice, and that's one compliment Nick never gets tired of hearing. After all, Stevie Wonder has won twenty-two Grammy Awards, recorded over thirty top-ten hits, won an Academy Award, and been inducted into the Rock and Roll Hall of Fame! Stevie, who has been blind since birth, signed with Motown Records when he was only twelve in 1962. Before he turned twenty, Stevie had a string of hit singles and was producing some of his own tracks. He fought hard to have full creative control over his music and eventually succeeded, which was unheard of during that time. In addition to singing, Stevie plays the piano, synthesizer, harmonica, congas, drums, bass guitar, organ, and clarinet. Stevie Wonder's music is so special because it appeals to such a wide audience. People of all ages, races, and walks of life are brought together by his catchy lyrics and smooth delivery. Bringing people together through music is what the Jonas Brothers are all about, so it's no wonder that they idolize Stevie Wonder.

THE RAMONES

The Ramones were a band from Queens, New York, that are regarded by most as the first-ever American punk rock band. Joey, Johnny, Tommy, and Dee Dee all changed their last names to Ramone and played their first gig in 1974. They toured almost nonstop for the next twenty-two years and developed a cult following. The style of the Ramones was totally unlike anything anyone had heard before. Their songs were short, very fast paced, and filled with frantic energy. The Jonas Brothers love their energetic, catchy music, and you can hear how the Ramones influenced the boys in songs like "Goodnight and Goodbye" and "Inseparable."

DAFT PUNK

Daft Punk is a band made up of two Paris house musicians (musicians who play music mixed with electronic sounds in nightclubs), Guy-Manuel de Homem-Christo and Thomas Bangalter. They are one of the most successful and critically acclaimed electronic music groups of all time. They mix techno, house, and electro styles to produce their own signature sound. They produce their own music videos and are able to procure some of the most talented directors in the world to work on them, including Spike Jonze, Michel Gondry, Roman Coppola, and Seb Janiak. The Jonas Brothers, particularly Nick, love Daft Punk's innovative use of electronic sounds and their high-energy dance tracks.

JOHN MAYER

When the Jonas Brothers need an escape from the chaos of touring or are nursing broken hearts, they pull up some John Mayer on their iPods and groove to his signature bluesy sound. John is a seriously talented guitar player. He started out performing acoustic rock, but eventually started singing the blues. He is famous for his quirky, clever lyrics, which really inspire Kevin, Joe, and Nick when they get stuck while working on a song. John has won multiple Grammy Awards, two for his 2006 album *Continuum* and the Song of the Year Award for his single "Daughters." John writes all of his own music, rocks the stage with killer guitar solos, and speaks out about the things he believes in—no wonder the Jonas boys look up to him!

THE POLICE

The Police, led by front man Sting, are a band that has had the long-lasting, innovative career the Jonas Brothers aspire to have. The Police are a British New Wave band that released five albums that burnt up the charts between 1978 and 1983. They mixed all sorts of sounds from the music scene at the time, including punk, reggae, rock, and pop (sound like anyone else we know?). The music of the Police is ageless, and their hits, like "Every Breath You Take" and "Don't Stand So Close to Me," are still played on radio stations across the country every day. The Police broke up after 1983, but in 2007 they reunited and went back on tour. I guess you can never know what the future holds for a band!

JOHNNY CASH

The Jonas Brothers love old music just as much

as the hottest new singles, and they listen to a lot of artists that no one would expect, like country legend Johnny Cash. Known as "the Man in Black," Cash has really inspired the brothers, especially when it comes to their fashion sense. Johnny was known for wearing lots of black, skinny ties, and tailored pants—just like the Jonas Brothers! Johnny wasn't your typical country singer. His songs were edgy and echoed themes of sorrow, morality, and redemption. He was way ahead of his time with his deep, gravelly voice and half-singing, half-speaking style of music. Johnny continued recording and performing until his death in 2003.

Now the only question is—which cool new bands are the Jonas Brothers influencing right now?

CHAPTER 14
FUN, FAST JONAS FACTS

So you think you're the Jonas Brothers' biggest fan? You have both of their albums, have been to every one of their concerts you could, have watched all of their music videos and home movies on youtube.com, and check their myspace.com page every day, right? Well, here are the key facts that any Jonas Brothers' fan should always have at the tips of their fingers!

KEVIN
FULL NAME: Paul Kevin Jonas II
NICKNAME: "Kev"
DATE OF BIRTH: November 5, 1987
PLACE OF BIRTH: Teaneck, New Jersey
HEIGHT: 5' 9"
STAR SIGN: Scorpio

HOBBIES: Playing guitar and bowling

INSTRUMENTS: Guitar

FAVORITE FOOD: Sushi

FAVORITE COLOR: Green

FAVORITE ICE CREAM: Rocky Road (especially with cookie dough and hot chocolate sauce)

FAVORITE SPORT: Pole vaulting

FAVORITE MOVIE: *About a Boy*

LUCKY NUMBER: Fifteen

IF HE WASN'T A MUSICIAN, HE'D LIKE TO BE: A race car driver

JOE

FULL NAME: Joseph Adam Jonas

NICKNAMES: "Joe" or "Danger"

DATE OF BIRTH: August 15, 1989

PLACE OF BIRTH: Casa Grande, Arizona

STAR SIGN: Leo

HOBBIES: Making movies, jogging, and working out

INSTRUMENTS: Guitar, piano, percussion (tambourine)

FAVORITE MOVIES: *Finding Neverland* and *Four Feathers*

FAVORITE FOOD: Chicken cutlet sandwich with mayo

FAVORITE COLOR: Blue

FAVORITE ICE CREAM: Chocolate marshmallow (especially with peanut butter mixed in)

FAVORITE SPORT: Wiffle ball

IF HE WASN'T A MUSICIAN, HE'D LIKE TO BE: A comedian

NICK

FULL NAME: Nicholas Jerry Jonas

NICKNAME: "Nick" or "Nicky" (but only to his family!)

DATE OF BIRTH: September 16, 1992

PLACE OF BIRTH: Dallas, Texas

HEIGHT: 5' 6"

STAR SIGN: Virgo

HOBBIES: Music, songwriting, baseball, collecting baseball cards, tennis, golf

INSTRUMENTS: Guitar, drums, piano

FAVORITE FOOD: Steak

FAVORITE DESSERT: Pumpkin pie

FAVORITE COLOR: Blue

FAVORITE ICE CREAM: Cotton candy

FAVORITE SPORT: Baseball

IF HE WASN'T A MUSICIAN, HE'D LIKE TO BE: A professional golfer or baseball player

FRANKIE

FULL NAME: Franklin Nathaniel Jonas

NICKNAMES: "Frankie" or "Frank the Tank"

DATE OF BIRTH: September 28, 2000

PLACE OF BIRTH: Wyckoff, New Jersey

STAR SIGN: Libra

HOBBIES: Riding his bike, wrestling with his brothers

INSTRUMENTS: He wants to play drums when he's old enough.

FAVORITE SPORT: Baseball

FAVORITE SPORTS TEAM: New York Yankees

WHAT HE WANTS TO BE WHEN HE GROWS UP: A Jonas Brother. He'd like to join his brothers' band!

CHAPTER 15
SURFING THE NET—JONAS STYLE

The Jonas Brothers are always on the move. With albums, touring, a television show, and a possible TV movie on their schedules, there's no telling where they'll be next or what they'll be doing! So if you want to keep up with these super-cute, super-busy brothers, here is a list of websites for ongoing updates on the Jonas Brothers!

The Jonas Brothers would want you to always be careful online. Never give out any sort of personal information—like your name, address, phone number, or the name of your school or sports team—and never try to meet someone in person that you met online. When you are surfing the net, you have to remember that not everything you read there is true. Lots of people are creating websites out there, and sometimes they create false information to make their sites more exciting. In fact, that's one of the Jonas Brothers' pet peeves. They hate it when people leave comments pretending to be them online, but unfortunately it does happen, so take online information with a grain of salt. And remember, never surf the web without your parents' permission. Can't find your favorite website? Websites come and go, so don't worry—there will be another one to replace it soon!

www.jonasbrothers.com

This is the Jonas Brothers' official site. It has updates on their projects and tours and an online shop where you can buy official JB gear!

www.youtube.com/JonasBrothersMusic

This is the official Jonas Brothers' portion of You Tube. You can check out all of the brothers' music videos plus funny videos that the brothers post themselves!

They post new stuff all the time, so check it often.

<u>www.myspace.com/JonasBrothers</u>

This is the Jonas Brothers' official MySpace page. The Jonas Brothers love MySpace. They check this page often for new friend requests and to leave messages for their fans. Check it out (with your parents' permission, of course) and add yourself to the Jonas Brothers' friend list!